Journey
to the
Light

Journey
to the
Light

Carmeline

© Copyright 2024 by Carmeline

ISBN:978-1-963735-02-4

All rights reserved. No part of this book may be reproduced or transmitted in any form or by any means, electronic or mechanical, including photocopying, recording, or by any information storage and retrieval system, without permission in writing from the copyright owner.

The views expressed in this work are solely those of the author and do not necessarily reflect the views of the publisher, and the publisher disclaims any responsibility for them.

To order additional copies of this book, contact:

Proisle Publishing Services LLC
39-67 58th Street, 1st floor
Woodside, NY 11377, USA
Phone: (+1 646-480-0129)
info@proislepublishing.com

This book is dedicated to all those who have
found the Light within because they
have dared to make the journey...

ACKNOWLEDGEMENT

My deep appreciation for and deeper gratitude to my sister and brother-in-law, Denyse and Daniel Marcinek, my cousin, Marie Brien, and my friend Nicki Modaber for their invaluable help in preparing the manuscript, and to my son, Charles Anthony Pusateri for his willingness to share his creative side and produce the images for this book, and to my husband, Vincent Pusateri, Jr., for providing the financial support and the workspace that it takes to produce a work of art.

Also, I would like to thank all those who provided the lessons for me to make the journey. They were my teachers.

TABLE OF CONTENTS

FREE SPIRIT	1
FRIENDS	2
WINTER'S PACE	3
A POET	4
AT THE OPENING OF "TREE WHISPERS"	5
CHANGE	6
SURRENDER	7
KAVITA	8
AN UNRELATED QUESTION	9
THE BONSAI TREE	11
A TRIBUTE TO	12
ALFRED E. MILLER	12
IMAGINE	14
EDUCATION IN DIVERSITY	15
AT THE VAN GOGH AND GAUGUIN EXHIBITION	16
TRANSITION	19
A WINTER MEMORY	20
MEMORIAL DAY–2006	23
ON HER FUNERAL DAY LOUISE HABETLER SCHWIETERT OCTOBER 21, 2004	24
PEACEMAKING DAY OCTOBER 6, 2001	25
WHAT IS A TONY BACINO?	26
THE KITCHEN	28
VALENTINE'S DAY	30

MARRIAGE PARTNER	32
A TEACHER/A HEROINE	33
SHATTERED DREAMS	40
STICKY PLACES	41
FACING AN UNWANTED CHALLENGE	42
RUNNING AWAY	43
RESTART	44
SEPTEMBER 12, 2001	45
THE GIRLS AT THE TOP OR NANCY	46
THE EPIPHANY JANUARY 6, 2007	47
A WORK IN PROGRESS	48
LIFE'S FINAL CHOICE	**50**
JOURNEY TO THE LIGHT	51
RESURRECTION MAN	54

FREE SPIRIT

I am free Spirit soaring high

not one sound uttered in the sky

of puff-white clouds and eagle birds

who fly with me and say no words

Now look at us see what we see

held up by air and flying free.

FRIENDS

F riends pass in and out of our lives,
at certain times, to be the things we need.

>A thought . . . . . . a smile,
>and in an instant
>we are together again.

FRIENDS are answers to loneliness.

>To help each other along the way—
>is the path of friendship.

>VILIJA
>—A friend can never be measured
>in time or space
>—only in the depth
>of the heart's remembrance.

WINTER'S PACE

I watch the snow
fall soundlessly
on the waiting earth

                    Droplets of frozen
                    white crystals spill
                    in steady streams

Snow, snow, snow
heaping upon itself
to form a coverlet
of pristine peace
creating winter's pace

                    It slows us down
                    halting our hurry
                    so that we can enjoy
                            Life
                    at a standstill.

A POET

A poet cannot be
ought but that.

For he only rhymes,
meters, cadences
and essences his life

AT THE OPENING OF "TREE WHISPERS"*

In a forest
of paper trees
a lone dancer
swirled and spun
gracefully

Flying through
the delicate leaves
stopping
for a moment
to paint
a single stroke of beauty
with her dainty hand
with her swaying body
with her soul

---

* "Tree Whispers" is an installation of an international collaboration involving paper, art and stories relating to trees as a symbol and resource. This poet has one of her most published poems, "Transformation," hanging in the collection on a paper made with her own hands.

CHANGE

Exchanging
one preference

for another

SURRENDER

To relinquish control

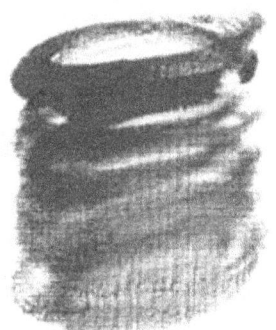

of the outcome

KAVITA

A poem has many mysteries

A poem has many joys

To find its inner essences

is not a game for girls and boys

So search your heart

And see the words

Not as they're written down

But as they're meant to help

You know that Life

Can never smile or frown

                                            Only you can do that!

AN UNRELATED QUESTION

What is peace . . .
    but the soft flowing of an unburdened mind
    free from the clutter of confusion and doubt

What is peace . . .
    but the quiet beating of a tranquil heart
        not tied to reason or emotion

What is peace . . .
    but the ability to remain in a state of joy
    when the facts would have it otherwise . . .

        So, if that's all that it is,

Why is it so difficult to maintain?

DIAMONDS IN THE SNOW

The glistening white of winter
makes diamonds
in the snow
sparkling bright,
twinkling light,
God's beauty
we can know

THE BONSAI TREE

Miniature of the real version
Every detail, every leaf
A perfect reproduction of the original

Trained to be small,
but great
in its
expression
of beauty

Who said
good things
don't come in
small packages?

A TRIBUTE TO ALFRED E. MILLER

Friendship knows no bounds
when it is blessed by Love.

It is always available when necessary.
Reliable when called upon.
Lavish in its scope.
Crossing every line
to provide
the foundation of its substance.

It is known,
to the participants
as a way of life,
of being loved,
of being cherished,
of being there.

Friendship is a way
of being connected to all good
of supporting one another's needs,
of co-starring in each other's lives.

When the role of friend
is played by a Master,
it energizes the relationship
and touches the world around it
with beauty and joy.

To be blessed by such as he
is truly a gift of God
—to always be treasured.

IMAGINE

Christmas in February
   with Valentines on the tree

Love combined with love
a cupid angel peeking
from a branch above
pink bows, red hearts
and twinkling hearts
and shining lights

        Imagine
   a sunrise or a sunset
        painting the sky
with colors of deep hue light
          touching light
     a cloud wispy and white
          Imagine

EDUCATION IN DIVERSITY

Diversity is a lesson that teaches us
about the hidden blessings of Life
We can learn so much from other's gifts,
if we could just
focus on them,
and not on our differences

We learn to work hard from our Polish citizens
We learn to persevere
and persist in any task
from our Mexican neighbors

We learn about community
from the Koreans and the Vietnamese,
and about family from the East Indians

Many of these values
were once part of the fabric of American life
Maybe these people have come
to remind us once again
of what was so important

AT THE VAN GOGH AND GAUGUIN EXHIBITION

We walk into the hall filled with silence
a fitting shrine to the genius of these two men
noticing at once the contrasting styles of their work
yet unmistakably Impressionistic in its direction

Eventually, our silent viewing is disturbed
by the bee-like buzzing of audio tapes
describing what we are looking at
as if we cannot understand it

Upon inquiring of one of the newly informed students
of these art treasures as to what had been learned
we discovered in their reply, "Nothing new"
and upon further investigation, "Nothing different, either"

So what was gained by this experience of something so true
that it was meant to touch the soul as the artist's gift to the viewer?
What was learned of the struggle between these two men
and the artistic expression that ruled their lives and their relationship?

Something subtle, about their work, about their lives
became apparent to us as we stood there absorbing
in our quiet contemplation
the paintings of these famous men
  —that they painted for the sake of painting

and not for our pleasure

Maybe that's the reason why enduring masterpieces are just that
because the artists aren't trying to please anyone,
not even themselves
they are reaching for something beyond themselves
trying to break through a limitation,
evolving their art to a new unfoldment

Someone has to do it, in order for mankind to progress
and that genius must work in the dark
in order to let the past go
sometimes without the compass of knowledge
as to what direction his work will take
to make us see and feel
what he has touched with his soul

It must be a lonely journey,
as evidenced by the struggle and remorse
and yet it is necessary
for the chosen one to take up the Cross
for without this courage and
its subsequent transformation of our past values
we could not go forward
into the light of greater Self-recognition

THE RED CARNATION

Love is so unexplainable
It has to be experienced to be felt

TRANSITION

Like fall,

                              transition

        is only a change in form

                giving hope

         to the resurgence of Life,

            as the seasons pass.

A WINTER MEMORY

Sparkling diamonds,

falling from the sky

through air so cold

it freezes them

into crystal hardness.

Some people

call this snow.

I feel it

touching my face

Cold, wet

On the warmth of my skin

it melts instantly,

a brief remembrance

of this beautiful sensation.

BOB AT THE CORE

Brings out the essence
of
beauty in everything

MUSIC AND BUTTERFLIES

Music and butterflies

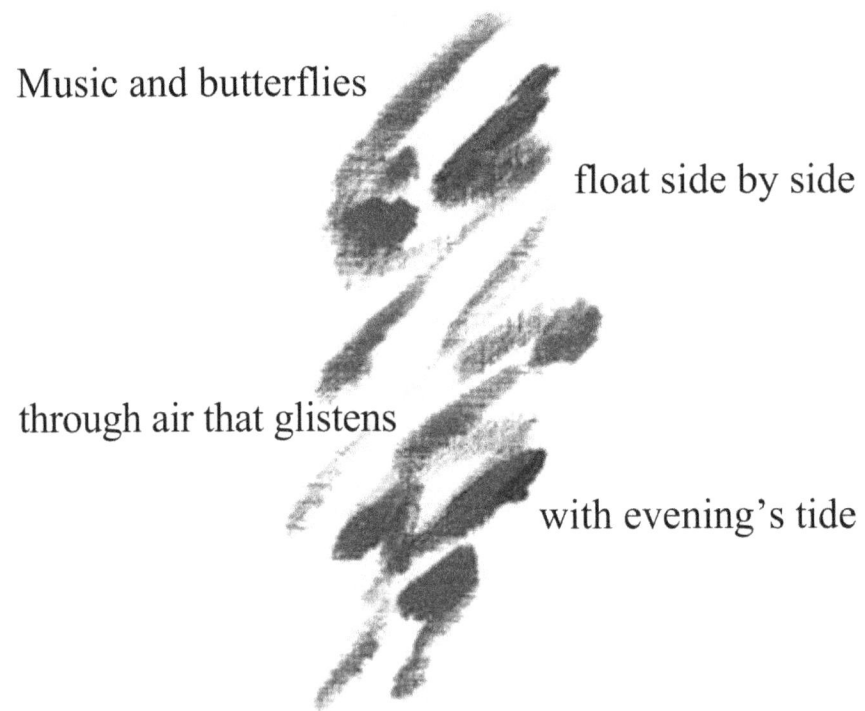

                    float side by side

through air that glistens

                    with evening's tide

MEMORIAL DAY–2006

Again we stand in tribute

No war yet won

No soldiers brought home alive

The flag flying over us

Red, white and blue

the Stars and Stripes

A symbol of our faithfulness

Be brave, my country Stand fast,

be proud to be an American

ON HER FUNERAL DAY LOUISE HABETLER SCHWIETERT OCTOBER 21, 2004

I weep silently for my friend whom I treasure
My tears will not make sound
The grief is trapped inside me
in chains of heartbreak
It is bound
No more to hear that voice or see that smile
No more to talk or linger over dinner for awhile
And yet her passing
has brought forth a gift,
a blessing on this day
to a new expression
of all that's been before
to a new-found entrance
    to an ever-open door
        And with this
        has our journey full-circle come
            As for once, and now forever
            we enter our true home
                    —the heart.

PEACEMAKING DAY OCTOBER 6, 2001

P^{eace} Is

a feeling

a process

a state of mind

a greeting/a goodbye and it's

where you're at

when you're

Who You Are

WHAT IS A TONY BACINO?

A continuous activity
moving all the time
A smile here and
then a frown
A keeping all in line

A steady beat of energy
for all who come to ask direction, meaning
or the way to do some heavy task

A question, then an answer
then a pondering until
a moment when decision is simply,
"Do my will"

It is not mere reflection that causes me today
to search for deeper meaning than the one that's come my way

Instead it is a yearning

to know the Truth of this

Without Tony Bacino

Life's message would be missed

It's the answer to a puzzle so rarely found because

The answer's very meaning is the puzzle's very cause.

THE KITCHEN

A gathering place
a meeting place
a greeting place
Once the hustle-bustle
of sitting altogether
fingers burned
on oven-hot casserole
milk spilling through
the crack of table leaf
     wailing
      laughing
silent praying

Then absent places
off to games of sport
games of love
games of chance
Who will sit together tonight?
      two
      three
one alone

Sometimes they come together again
joined by others
use the larger table trade stories
share ideas play games
drink coffee, eat chocolate wild confusion

             The table's pushed back now
                          set for three
             sometimes only two quiet,
                          peaceful

             Noise and laughter on the stoop door opens,
             home once more one, two, three
             the "single's scene"
      my kitchen gate
  replaced by a revolving door

      Day and night
the kitchen's bursting at the seams
                          My head is too

             And now,
                   the kitchen grows dark in the twilight,
                          waiting

        How many plates do I Set tonight?

VALENTINE'S DAY

We remember love in our thoughts
as a feeling,
as a longing,
as a fulfillment.

Not often as an action,
more as a reaction
More how we reacted to
or felt when we were kissed
than the kiss itself.

We remember someone saying "I love you," and
how our heart skipped a beat
and we felt safe inside.

But Love itself is a state of being
having more to do
with how the one who is loving
is feeling and
what they are transmitting.

As they splatter you with good will,
you are energized and made whole.

Any sense of anything other than well-being is obliterated
and all that you are left with
is Love's Radiance
to bask in
to glow in
to feel

LEADERSHIP

It's hard being a leader

People

        tend to want to follow you,

            instead of

        where you're leading them

        which is to that place within

where they can find themselves

MARRIAGE PARTNER

I am the mahogany of your life
I am the one who
will not warp or twist
in the winds of change
or split in two
when tested
by the extremes of the world.

I am the solid
the strong
the stable,
the protection
against the elements
that would damage our union.

I am not here for myself
but to provide the strength
for all of us
to endure.

My presence is the foundation
upon which
we build our family
and through which
we express our love.

A TEACHER/A HEROINE

Early in life,
when she decided
to be a teacher of children
who would set their minds free
She had no idea
what she would endure
to make sure that
their learning would be secure
How many times on every occasion
did she turn conflict to peace
without words of abrasion
How many times
did she follow her heart
to give a young person
a new and fresh start
And now that her work
has come to an end
we gather to honor
our colleague and friend
Her life's been a tribute
She's given her best
and blazed a new trail for all of the rest
God bless you and keep you
as you go on your way
Let every tomorrow be a wonderful day

EXPECTATION

The illusion of a delusion

HUMANITY

There's no escaping it—
we're all in this world together

DISCOMFORT

A willingness

to grow

GROWTH

When Life doesn't fit and
you need a new pair of shoes

DELUSION

Too many times,
we have expectations
that something we want
to happen, can happen

By the time
we find out this isn't possible,
we have discovered
a new expectation,
 and once again,

—fooled our self.

MINDSET

See them,
looking through concrete eyes
and formed faces

Thoughts set
in stony rigidity.
Calloused minds, hardened
to the refreshing softness
of new light, new ideas
a new perspective

SHATTERED DREAMS

They break apart
like shards of glass
puzzle pieces that
no longer fit the whole

Strewn about
unrecognizable
from what kept them together
with Life's glue

Letting go
tears at the heart
broken by frustration and remorse
What happened, speaks the mind?

No answers come.
But surely
there must be a reason
for this deliberate loss
What did I do, asks the soul?

Nothing, nothing.
This is merely the rearranging
of the patterns that will weave together
—a better you.

STICKY PLACES

In the process of discovering

who we are

without affixing our ambitions to a star

We come upon areas

in Life which could be called

the sticky places

They are neither here nor there

neither attainable nor avoidable

not permanent or temporary

not favored or disliked

Just something we know has to change

in order for us

to move on with it.

FACING AN UNWANTED CHALLENGE

It comes to every soul
to test its mettle
a task not chosen
a lifestyle unwanted
a mission impossible
to determine
what choice will be made

If it were easy,
what one wanted,
there would be no tempering
of the will, no flexing
of the moral muscle

One could be left alone
to wriggle out of the difficulty
instead of having to proceed
and do what needs to be done

Facing the challenge, at least,
you know you're with God
Who else could help you through this?

RUNNING AWAY

What are we running from?
as fast as our legs can carry us
Are we running from commitment?
from loneliness
from love

Where are our legs taking us?
to confusion to chaos
to escape

From what?
the pain
the unhappiness the loneliness

Do we think
if we run fast enough
it won't catch up ?
it won't touch us
it won't hurt us
If we run,
are we going anywhere?
are we going anywhere at all?

RESTART

To begin again,

after waiting so long,

becomes more of a journey

than I bargained for

So

it's back to one day at a time

one foot in front of the other

and

Just starting again,

before

waiting

some

more.

SEPTEMBER 12, 2001

The sky was empty

There were no planes

in the cloudless sky

We were used to hearing

the jet roar sounds

Seeing the streaming whiteness

trailing the airplane

Today, the sky was empty

like a ghost town

like a deserted island

Not dotted with the caravan of planes

Making their way to waiting airports

No, today, the sky was empty

Something had happened to America

THE GIRLS AT THE TOP OR NANCY

It's such a heavy burden
to always be right
or always be
anything
but not so hard to always be

Trust this
and you will see amazing things
begin to happen
right before your very eyes
as each person you meet
begins to pull at your ball of yarn
and unravel the round and about strings of Life
so that you cannot just see them,
but be them too.

"Twinkle, twinkle, little star"
how I wonder that you are
So big
So magnificent
So far

"Oh say, can you see"
That your yarn and mine
Are knitted together
into Ecstasy

THE EPIPHANY
JANUARY 6, 2007

In the silence of my own heart
I feel the peace
that passeth understanding

I know
that all my problems have been solved
that all my traumas have been laid to rest
No more
do I struggle
or strain for perfection
I can let it all go
all that has ever troubled me
for solution somewhere else

Is peace only the absence of conflict
or is it also the recognition of well-being
and the happiness that comes
from living a life of contentment

Blessed be God! Blessed be His Holy Name!

A WORK IN PROGRESS

What I've learned in sixty years
is to be wise
Wisdom surpasses cleverness

What I've learned in sixty years
is to be grateful
Gratitude dispels poverty

As I continue to move on through Life's journey
of this "parenthesis in Eternity"
I see myself undoing patterns learned from the beginning
that hinder my true identity

This year of sixty
is the start of maturity
It is a way of taking all the essentials
that are incorporated into my soul
and making them useful
in my experience

It is a way of determining
just how far I have come in being
a self-determined individual

Can I now risk being myself

having what I want
fulfilling my needs
In spite of others' parameters for me

Or must I chip away
more of the marbleized outer shell
that has defined my personality,
which most consider to be my soul

A fitting initiation,
for the testing ground of the decade to come.
Dipping one value at a time
into the waters of validation,
to purify what I have become
in this lifetime.
Still, a work in progress.

LIFE'S FINAL CHOICE

In the middle of this island
in my mind
I encounter Death

It says choose.
This side
or
the other
How do you want to play it?

Dead or alive?
Awake or asleep?

I don't know.
Do I have to answer yet?

Can't it wait
until tomorrow?

JOURNEY TO THE LIGHT

Mostly small steps
not often large strides
sometimes unnoticeable progress
our journey to the Light

>Why such a lengthy process?
>no quick accomplishment
>no immediate satisfaction

An adverse transit to
unfathomable depths
Made even more arduous,
by the mistakes of the human self

>Is it possible to even complete the trip?
>Can one make it in
>a lifetime?
>Oh yes, as one has the realization
>that the journey
>only takes us a short distance

—to the Self-within

GRATITUDE

A deep feeling we have

when,

without deserving it,

we know we've

been blessed.

APPRECIATION

A deep feeling we have

when we recognize the excellence in us,

is in others as well

RESURRECTION MAN

Break through
O, splendor of my soul
Release the shackles
of my humanhood
that served to entomb me
as I struggled
through the lessons of this life
This human journey
has tempered my will
like fire does steel
strengthening me
to break through
the barriers of my ego's hold

Relentlessly, it sabotaged
my efforts
as I tried to persist
But I fought on
with much to lose
And finally I did lose—

I lost my life

—only to gain my soul.

www.ingramcontent.com/pod-product-compliance
Lightning Source LLC
LaVergne TN
LVHW050026080526
838202LV00069B/6931